THAWED

THAWED

a collegiate guide to food

recipes and photographs by Christine Ravago
edited by Kristi Laurenz

iUniverse, Inc.
New York Lincoln Shanghai

Thawed
A Collegiate Guide To Food

iUniverse, Inc.

For information address:

iUniverse, Inc.
2021 Pine Lake Road, Suite 100
Lincoln, NE 68512
www.iuniverse.com

ISBN: 0-595-32401-0 (Pbk)
ISBN: 0-595-66552-7 (Cloth)

Printed in the United States of America

contents

preface

Cooking—it's the one thing we leave home knowing little about. And they wonder why college campuses are a major driving force behind Ramen noodles and Easy Mac sales. What I hope to share in this book is a basic introduction to food and cooking for the newly independent. That, however, is only the first lesson. What I hope to ultimately bring to your table is a valuable means for networking, friendship, and happiness.

If you cook it, they will come. Every college student is hungry. Sure, home cooked meals may seem daunting in comparison to the usual late night pizza. As appetizing as a greasy slice of pizza may sound, what I've learned is that college is about building friendships and challenging yourself.

There's nothing more memorable than six of your closest friends, juicy steaks, a bottle of cheap red wine, a roundtable discussion of the scandalous stories from the night before and unbearable laughter that confirms absolute satisfaction felt by those around you. I warn that once you've taken the time to explore the world of food and cooking, that feeling of utter and complete satisfaction is addictive.

glossary

beat—To stir ingredients rapidly.

blend—To combine ingredients using an electric blender.

boil—To heat a liquid until bubbles rise to the surface.

bone—To remove bones from any type of meat.

brown—To cook food in a pre-heated pan over a stove set at a high temperature, causing browning of the food's surface.

chop—To cut food into bite-size pieces using a knife. Chopped food is coarser than minced food.

cube—To slice food, making ½-inch cubes. Cubed food is larger than diced food.

dice—To slice food, making ¼-inch cubes.

fry—To immerse food in hot oil over high heat until cooked. Frying requires more oil than sautéing.

grate—To shred food into small particles by rubbing it against a serrated surface called a grater.

marinate—To soak a food, usually for more than a couple of hours, in a liquid mixture of seasonings called a marinade. Marinating is done in a glass or ceramic container, never in aluminum.

mince—To slice food into tiny pieces. Minced food is smaller than chopped food.

sauté—To cook food in a small amount of oil in a shallow pan over high heat, usually requiring little cooking time.

season—To improve the taste of food by adding spices or various flavors.

seed—To remove the seeds from foods.

simmer—To cook food over a stove set at a medium-low temperature so that tiny bubbles rise to the surface.

dinner menus

To help you get started, I've grouped together some of the recipes from this book and paired them with wines as ideas for dinner menus. The recipes generally serve 4 to 6 people.

buying food

beef	Look for beef cuts stamped "U.S. INSP'D & P'S'D." This means the meat was federally inspected for wholesomeness.
USDA Prime	Prime roasts and steaks are best prepared by roasting and broiling. Prime beef is tender, juicy, and flavorful. Its marbling enhances flavor and juiciness.
USDA Choice	Choice beef from the loin and ribs are tender, juicy, and flavorful and are recommended for roasting and broiling. The same is true for rump, round, and blade chuck cuts.
USDA Select	Select beef is leaner than the higher grades. With less marbling, it can lack the juiciness and flavor of higher grades. Tender cuts can be roasted or broiled but less tender cuts should be marinated.
lamb	Always try to buy USDA-graded lamb. Lamb cuts have the same characteristics as prime and choice beef. Most cuts of these grades are tender and may be oven roasted, broiled, or pan-broiled.
USDA Choice or Prime	Choice or prime grade leg of lamb is great when oven roasted. Less tender cuts are best slowly braised (meat is first browned, then cooked, tightly covered, in a small amount of liquid at low heat for a lengthy period of time).
pork	USDA grades for pork reflect two levels of quality—USDA (Prime and Choice) and Acceptable or Unacceptable. Look for cuts with a small amount of fat over the outside and a grayish pink color. The meat should also have some marbling.

seafood	Don't buy frozen seafood above the frost line in the grocer's freezer. If you see frozen seafood with signs of frost, the seafood may have been stored too long or has been thawed and refrozen.
chicken	Color is not an indicator for flavor or fat content. Rather, differences in the color of chicken meat are a result of the chicken's diet. The most important criteria for selecting chicken should be the "Sell By" date on the package. Fresh chicken should not have a detectable odor, and the flesh should feel firm.

storing food

raw foods

To prevent food poisoning, make sure raw foods are tightly contained and stored on the bottom shelf of the refrigerator to avoid dripping.

canned goods

Never store canned goods directly in the refrigerator once opened. Instead, place contents in a plastic or glass container and use refrigerated contents within 2 days.

perishable foods

Throw away any perishable foods left at room temperature for more than 5 hours. Store leftovers in the refrigerator and eat within 2 days.

seafood

Keep seafood in the coldest part of the refrigerator or freezer immediately after buying. Discard shellfish if the shells crack easily. Thaw seafood in the refrigerator overnight. If you need to thaw seafood quickly, use a microwave. Also, cook fish so that the fat drips away, and don't use the drippings.

suggested storage times for raw meat

	freezer (0° F)	refrigerator (40° F)
Beef roasts and steaks	6–12 months	3–5 days
Beef and lamb, ground	3–4 months	1–2 days
Lamb roasts and chops	6–9 months	3–5 days
Pork roasts and chops	4–6 months	3–5 days
Chicken pieces or whole	9–12 months	1–2 days

grilling

direct grilling   Arrange coals evenly in a single layer, placed as far as 1 inch beyond the area of the food.

indirect grilling   Use a large disposable foil pan and place it in the center of the firebox. Arrange the coals around the pan.

lighting coals   After adding lighter fluid according to package directions, let stand 1 minute and then ignite with a match. Never add more lighter fluid after the fire has started. Once lit, allow the coals to heat for 20–30 minutes or until ash gray or glowing red at night before grilling.

flare-ups   Flare-ups happen when meat juices drip into the coals and can result in burned meat. Lower the heat by raising the grill rack and spreading the coals. For major flare-ups, remove the meat from the grill and mist the flames with a water-spray bottle. Once the flames die down, you can continue grilling. Don't mist flare-ups on a gas grill. Instead, close the lid and wait for the flare-up to die down.

appetizers

¼ cup mayonnaise
1 package (8 ounces) cream cheese,
    room temperature
½ cup Parmesan cheese, grated
1 garlic clove, minced
1 teaspoon dried basil
1 can (14 ounces) artichoke hearts,
    drained and chopped
½ cup frozen spinach, slightly thawed and chopped
¼ cup mozzarella, grated
1 teaspoon salt
1 teaspoon pepper
crackers (to serve)

the dip

Blend mayonnaise, cream cheese, Parmesan cheese, garlic,
and basil.
Add artichoke and spinach and mix well.
Pour mixture in a shallow oven-safe dish and top with
mozzarella, salt, and pepper.
Bake in 350-degree oven for 25 minutes or until top is
lightly browned.
Serve with crackers.
Serves 6.

6 eggs, hard-boiled and cooled
1 tablespoon mustard
2 tablespoons mayonnaise
½ teaspoon garlic salt
Spanish paprika (garnish)

Spanish eggs

Remove egg shells, cut eggs lengthwise in half, carefully
remove the yolks, and put the yolks in a mixing
bowl.
Mix mustard, mayonnaise, and garlic salt with yolks and
spoon into hollowed egg whites.
Sprinkle with paprika and serve cool.
Serves 6.

2 very ripe plantains, peeled
6 tablespoons vegetable oil
brown sugar (to sprinkle)
maple syrup (to drizzle)

sweet nanas

Slice plantains into thirds and then slice each section
    lengthwise in half.
Heat oil in pan over medium heat and add plantain slices.
Fry plantains until bright yellow in color and soft.
Transfer to plate, sprinkle with brown sugar, drizzle with
    syrup, and serve.
Serves 4.

2 cups Bisquick
¾ cup milk
1 cup sharp cheddar cheese, grated
4 tablespoons butter, room temperature
½ teaspoon garlic powder
½ teaspoon dried thyme

easy cheesy

In a mixing bowl, mix Bisquick, milk, and cheese.
Form roughly-shaped biscuit mounds and place 1 inch apart
    on a greased baking sheet.
Melt butter and add seasonings.
Brush seasoned butter on biscuits and bake in 450-degree
    oven for 12 minutes.
Makes 12 biscuits.

3 eggs
3 tablespoons vanilla extract
1½ cups oil
2 cups sugar
3 cups flour
1 teaspoon salt
1 teaspoon cinnamon
1 teaspoon baking soda
¼ teaspoon baking powder
2 zucchinis, grated
½ cup pecans, halved

zucchini nut loaf

In large bowl, blend eggs, vanilla extract, and oil.
In another bowl, combine sugar, flour, salt, cinnamon,
        baking soda, and baking powder.
Slowly add flour mixture to large bowl.
Add zucchini and pecans.
Pour batter into greased bread loaf pan.
Bake in 350-degree oven for 1 hour.
Serves 12.

1 onion, diced
6 slices bacon
1 garlic clove, minced
2 tablespoons chicken broth
2 cups water
2 medium potatoes, cubed
1½ cups (2 medium-size links) spicy sausage,
    cooked
1 cup cabbage, sliced
2 cups milk

comfort soup

Place onions and bacon in a deep saucepan and cook over
medium heat until onions are translucent.
Remove bacon and crumble.
Add garlic to the onions and cook another minute.
Add broth, water, and potatoes and simmer for 15 minutes.
Add crumbled bacon, sausage, cabbage, and milk.
Cover and simmer for 5 minutes and serve.
Serves 6.

1 onion, minced
2 garlic cloves, minced
3 tablespoons olive oil
1 pound various mushrooms, washed and
    chopped
1¼ cups milk
3¼ cups vegetable broth
3 tablespoons butter, melted
fresh basil, chopped (for taste)
1 tablespoon salt
1 teaspoon pepper
1 cup favorite white cheese, grated

mushroom stew

In deep saucepan, sauté onions and garlic in oil over medium
      heat until golden.
Add bite-size mushrooms to pan and stir for 1 minute.
Add milk to pan, bring to a boil, and simmer for 5 minutes.
Add vegetable broth, butter, basil, salt, and pepper.
Let simmer for 12 minutes, plate individual servings, and top
      with grated cheese.
Serves 6.

4 sweet potatoes, boiled and mashed
1 cup sugar
2 eggs
½ cup milk
½ teaspoon salt
4 tablespoons butter, melted
1 teaspoon vanilla extract

topping:
   1 cup brown sugar
   ½ cup flour
   8 tablespoons butter, room temperature
   1 cup pecans, chopped

sweetie pie

In a large mixing bowl, mix together sweet potatoes, sugar, eggs, milk, salt, butter, and vanilla.

Pour mixture into a 2-quart greased glass casserole.

Mix together all topping ingredients and crumble topping evenly over potato mixture.

Bake in 350-degree oven for 35 - 45 minutes, uncovered.

Serves 6.

2 pounds beef sirloin, cubed 1 - 2 inches
1 large onion, sliced in wedges
4 tablespoons olive oil
2 teaspoons salt
1 teaspoon pepper
1 tablespoon dried rosemary
¼ cup flour
2 cups beef broth
1 can (11.2 ounces) Guinness beer
1¼ cups water
2 carrots, peeled and cubed
2 medium potatoes, peeled and cubed
1 package (10 ounces) frozen mixed
    vegetables

goodness stew

In a deep pot, sauté sirloin and onion in olive oil until
   browned.
Add salt, pepper, and rosemary and remove pan from heat.
Add flour and stir to coat evenly. Return to heat, stirring for
   2 minutes.
Add broth and Guinness and simmer for 45 minutes slightly
   uncovered, stirring occasionally.
Add carrots, ¾ cup of water, and potatoes, cover, and cook
   over low heat for 20 minutes.
Add frozen vegetables and ½ cup of water, raise stove
   temperature, and simmer for 15 minutes.
Serves 6.

main courses

beef
pork
lamb
seafood

1 cup soy sauce
½ cup honey
4 cuts ribeye steak
8 tablespoons fresh rosemary
2 teaspoons salt
1 teaspoon pepper
1 cup brown sugar

famous steak marinade

In a small dish, mix soy sauce and honey and set aside.
Cut deep slits through the center of the steaks and insert
      chopped rosemary in slits to ensure a flavorful steak.
Season the steaks with salt and pepper, then rub the steak
      with brown sugar, coating heavily.
Place steaks in a flat container and pour soy sauce marinade
      over the cuts.
Cover, refrigerate, and marinate overnight.
Cook in oven broiler or on outdoor grill.
Serves 4.

2 - 3 pounds beef pot roast
1 can (10.5 ounces) beef broth
2 teaspoons salt
¼ teaspoon pepper
½ teaspoon fresh rosemary, chopped
4 carrots, chopped lengthwise
2 white onions, whole
¼ cup cornstarch
¼ cup water

pot roast

In a deep pot, brown beef on both sides.
Pour in beef broth, cover, and cook for 2 hours over low
heat.
Add salt, pepper, rosemary, carrots, and onions. Cook
covered for another ½ hour.
Remove beef and vegetables from pot and place on a serving
dish.
Blend cornstarch and water.
Stir cornstarch mixture into pan juices until gravy thickens.
Season with additional salt and pepper, if needed.
Serves 6.

2 tablespoons olive oil
2 pounds sirloin steak, cubed
1 pound ground beef
12 ounces spicy sausage, cubed
1 large onion, cubed
¼ cup chili powder
1 teaspoon dried basil
1 teaspoon garlic salt
2 teaspoons cumin
2 cans (14.5 ounces) beef broth
2 cans (14.5 ounces) whole tomatoes, drained
1 cinnamon stick
3 bay leaves
3 jalapeños, sliced in half and seeded
½ cup cilantro, chopped
3 tablespoons cornmeal

chili

Heat oil over medium heat in a large pot.
Brown sirloin and spoon into bowl, leaving juices in pot.
Brown ground beef, sausage, and onions.
Add browned sirloin and remaining ingredients.
Simmer for 2 hours.
Before serving, remove bay leaves, cinnamon stick, and
      jalapeños.
Serves 6.

4 pork chops
1 onion, quartered
½ teaspoon salt
1 cup white rice, cooked
1 can (11 ounces) tomato bisque soup
11 ounces water

chops

Brown pork chops in sauté pan.
Place chops in oven-safe casserole dish.
Place a slice of onion on top of each chop and sprinkle with
       salt and rice over top.
Pour soup and water over chops.
Cover with foil and bake in 350-degree oven for 1 hour.
Serves 4.

½ cup ketchup
1 can (12 ounces) lemon-lime soda
1 garlic clove, minced
½ cup brown sugar
1 teaspoon salt
1 teaspoon pepper
1 pound pork (or chicken),
    cut into 1 x 2-inch pieces

pork kabobs

In a large container, mix marinade ingredients.
Add pork (chicken) to marinade and store covered in
refrigerator overnight.
Skewer on barbeque sticks and grill until done.
Serves 4.

rack of lamb, fat trimmings saved
2 tablespoons butter
1 carrot, diced
1 onion, diced
1 celery stalk, diced
1 garlic clove, minced
1 bay leaf
3 tablespoons dried thyme
3¼ cups water
1 teaspoon salt
1 teaspoon pepper
½ cup orange zest
½ cup sugar
½ cup breadcrumbs

merry lamb

In medium saucepan, melt ½ of butter and cook meat
trimmings, carrot, onion, celery, garlic, bay leaf, and
thyme until trimmings are browned.
Pour 3 cups of water into the pan and simmer for 30
minutes.
Add remaining butter, salt, and pepper to broth.
Stir broth, discard meat trimmings, and set broth aside.
In another pan, add orange zest, sugar, and ¼ cup of water
and bring to a boil.
Cook for about 4 minutes and remove from stove.
Combine zest with breadcrumbs.
Rub lamb with ½ of breadcrumb mixture, place on greased
roasting pan, and cook in 400-degree oven for 30
minutes.
Turn the lamb rack over, sprinkle the remaining
breadcrumbs, and cook for another 30 minutes.
Place lamb rack on a serving dish, drizzle warm broth over
lamb, and serve.
Serves 6.

1 pint heavy whipping cream
1 cup cooking sherry
1 garlic clove, minced
1 teaspoon salt
1 teaspoon pepper
12 ounces cheese tortellini, cooked
12 ounces smoked salmon, torn into bite-size
    pieces
¾ cup green peas

tortellini salmon bake

In sauté pan, let cream and sherry simmer over medium-high
     heat while stirring for 15 minutes.
Add remaining ingredients and cook for 10 minutes.
Serves 6.

vegetarian

3 tablespoons olive oil
1 onion, minced
2 garlic cloves, minced
4 tablespoons dried basil
1 can (15 ounces) pumpkin pie filling
1 teaspoon salt
1 teaspoon pepper
1 teaspoon nutmeg
1 cup vegetable broth
1 cup heavy whipping cream
9 ounces fettuccini, cooked

pumpkin alfredo

Heat olive oil in large sauté pan over medium-low heat.
Add the onion, garlic, and basil and cook for 5 minutes.
Add pumpkin, salt, pepper, and nutmeg and cook for 5
     minutes.
Add broth to pan and bring to a boil.
Cover and let simmer for 10 minutes.
Stir cream into pumpkin mixture and spoon sauce onto
     cooked fettuccini.
Serves 4.

3 tablespoons olive oil
1½ cups broccoli florets
2 tablespoons water
¾ cup carrots, sliced lengthwise
1½ cups snow peas, ends trimmed
6 fresh shitake mushrooms, slivered
½ cup water chestnuts, drained and sliced
1 garlic clove, minced
½ teaspoon ginger, minced
4 tablespoons soy sauce
3 tablespoons vegetable broth
1 teaspoon cornstarch

springtime stir-fry

Heat oil in wok (or deep frying pan) over medium heat.
Increase the heat to medium-high and add the broccoli and
    water.
Cook broccoli for 3 minutes or until bright green.
Add the carrots, snow peas, mushrooms, water chestnuts,
    garlic, and ginger.
Stir-fry for 10 minutes or until the vegetables are crisp-tender.
In a small bowl, combine the soy sauce, broth, and
    cornstarch and mix well until smooth.
Add sauce to the wok and stir-fry for about 5 minutes.
Serves 6.

4 eggplants, cut into 2-inch cubes and covered
    with salted water for 30 minutes
4 potatoes, cubed
2 green bell peppers, cubed
1 large onion, cubed
3 summer squash, cubed
3 tomatoes, cubed
½ pound fresh green beans, halved
½ pound mushrooms, halved
1 bulb garlic, separated and peeled
2 tablespoons dried oregano
2 tablespoons fresh basil, chopped
½ can (15 ounces) tomato sauce
¼ cup and 2 tablespoons olive oil
2 teaspoons salt
2 teaspoons pepper
¼ cup water

all-veggie casserole

Drain and rinse the eggplant, then combine it with other
chopped vegetables, garlic, oregano, and basil and
place into a 3 x 13 x 18-inch roasting pan.
Pour the tomato sauce, olive oil, salt, and pepper over the
vegetables.
Cover pan with foil and bake in 375-degree oven for 1 hour,
adding ¼ cup of water about halfway through
cooking to keep moist.
Serves 6.

1 pound fresh spinach
9 ounces ricotta cheese
1 egg
2 teaspoons fennel seed
½ cup Parmesan cheese, grated
1 teaspoon salt
1 teaspoon pepper
½ cup flour
1 tablespoon dried thyme
5 tablespoons butter, melted
2 garlic cloves, minced

spinach cakes

Cook spinach in covered saucepan until fully wilted.
Place in colander, let drain, and cool.
Squeeze out excess water.
Add ricotta cheese, egg, fennel seed, Parmesan cheese, salt,
and pepper.
Spoon about 4 tablespoons of mixture and form into a patty.
Coat with flour and season with thyme.
Continue process with the rest of the mixture.
Fill a large skillet half full with water and bring to a boil.
Carefully place cakes in water and cook for 5 minutes on each
side.
In a saucepan, melt butter, add garlic, and spoon over cooked
spinach cakes.
Makes 4 to 5 spinach cakes.

chicken

1 cup bread crumbs
2 teaspoons salt
¼ cup Parmesan cheese, grated
1 cup milk
3 large chicken breasts, halved
1 cup cooking oil
2 tablespoons butter
3 tablespoons olive oil
2 tablespoons flour
1 garlic clove, minced
¼ cup water
½ cup white wine
1 cup half and half
¼ cup sour cream
1 cup mild asiago cheese, grated
¼ teaspoon fresh basil, chopped
3 cups bowtie pasta, cooked
6 broccoli florets, lightly steamed
6 white mushrooms, lightly steamed

Parmesan chicken

Combine breadcrumbs, 1 teaspoon of salt, and Parmesan
cheese.
Pour milk in dish.
Dip chicken in breadcrumbs, then in milk, and then back in
breadcrumbs.
Heat oil in frying pan over medium heat and fry chicken until
golden.
Drain over paper towels.
In a saucepan over medium heat, add butter, olive oil, and
flour and stir until well blended.
Then add garlic, water, 1 teaspoon of salt, wine, half and half,
sour cream, grated cheese, and basil and stir until
melted.
Remove sauce from heat.
Place 1 cup of pasta in each serving size bowl.
Spoon sauce over pasta and top with chicken, broccoli, and
mushrooms.
Serves 3.

2 pounds chicken wings
1 cup brown sugar
½ cup vinegar
¼ cup lemon-lime soda
2 garlic cloves, minced
2 tablespoons soy sauce
1 teaspoon pepper
2 cups white rice, cooked

brown sugar babies

Place chicken in oven-safe casserole.
In a bowl, mix remaining ingredients and pour over chicken.
Cover with foil and cook in 300-degree oven for 1½ hours.
Serve over rice.
Serves 4.

6 boneless chicken thighs
½ cup olive oil
1 can (28 ounces) whole tomatoes,
    strained and quartered
1 cup pesto sauce
12 slices French bread
1 cup Parmesan cheese, grated
½ cup pine nuts

Italian meal

Preheat oven to broil setting.
Place oil-brushed chicken in a single layer in a deep roasting
pan and broil for 15 minutes.
While broiling, turn chicken over and remove when golden
brown.
Pour out excess fat drippings.
Top chicken with tomatoes and half of pesto sauce and broil
chicken for 10 more minutes.
Spread remaining pesto on bread.
Arrange bread over chicken, sprinkle with Parmesan cheese
and pine nuts, and broil for 5 minutes.
Serves 6.

4 large chicken thighs, skinned
4 tablespoons flour
1 tablespoon dijon mustard
6 tablespoons olive oil
2 tablespoons butter
2 small onions, sliced into wedges
2½ cups light beer
2 tablespoons Worcestershire sauce
1 teaspoon salt
1 teaspoon pepper

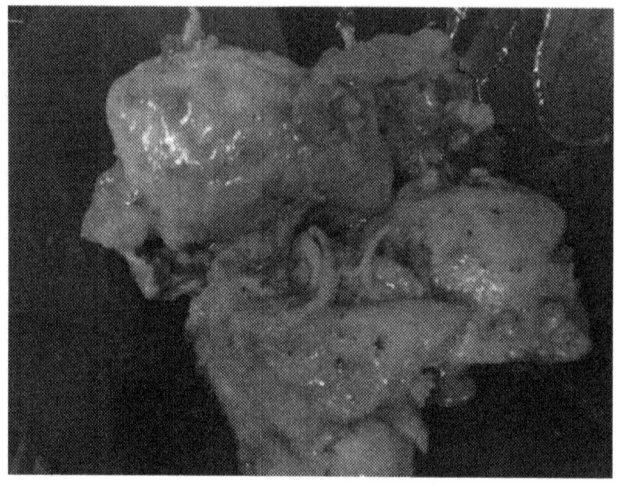

beer-stewed wings

Coat chicken in flour.
In large skillet, heat mustard, olive oil, and butter over
    medium-high heat.
Add chicken and cook until golden brown.
Remove chicken from skillet and sauté onions until
    translucent.
Add the chicken, beer, Worcestershire sauce, salt, and
    pepper.
Bring to a boil and simmer uncovered for 45 minutes, stirring
    occasionally, until chicken is tender.
Serves 4.

8 tablespoons flour
5 tablespoons cornstarch
5 tablespoons sugar
2 teaspoons salt
4 eggs
¼ cup sesame seeds
¼ cup green onions, chopped (optional)
2 pounds small chicken wings or
      6 large drumsticks
cooking oil

sweet n' crispy battered chicken

Mix batter ingredients in large container.
Add chicken to batter and store covered in refrigerator
    overnight.
Fill deep frying pan ¼ full with oil and heat to medium-high.
When oil is hot, fry wings until golden brown.
Serves 6.

4 tablespoons olive oil
2 pounds chicken meat, cubed
2 garlic cloves, minced
1 tablespoon mild curry powder
1 teaspoon pepper
1¼ cups mayonnaise
2 tablespoons honey
1 tablespoon dried basil

not-so-curry chicken

Heat oil in large skillet over medium-high heat.
Add chicken, garlic, and curry powder and cook until chicken
    is no longer pink.
Discard pan juices, transfer chicken to a bowl, and let chicken
    cool completely in refrigerator.
Add pepper, mayonnaise, honey, and basil and mix well.
Serves 6.

5 tablespoons maple syrup
2 tablespoons sugar
1 orange peel, grated
1 orange, juiced
3 tablespoons ketchup
2 teaspoons Worcestershire sauce
6 boneless chicken thighs

maple-grilled chicken

Mix marinade ingredients.
Add chicken to marinade, cover, and refrigerate for 30
    minutes.
Grill chicken for approximately 10 - 20 minutes using indoor
    or outdoor grill.
Cut through center of chicken to ensure the meat is fully
    cooked.
Baste chicken with leftover marinade while grilling.
Serves 6.

desserts

filling:

    12 graham cracker wafers, smashed

    2 cups brown sugar

    3 tablespoons butter, room temperature

    2 cups crunchy peanut butter

coating:

    ½ block (2 ounces) Gulf wax

    1 bag (11 ounces) butterscotch chips or
        chocolate chips

peanut butter balls

Mix filling ingredients and refrigerate for 1 hour.
In double broiler, melt wax completely over medium heat.
Add chips to broiler and melt. Reduce heat to low and let sit
    for 5 minutes.
Form chilled filling into 1½-inch diameter balls and dip into
    coating using a spoon.
Drop coated balls onto wax paper or foil and let harden.
Double coat if needed.
Serve chilled.
Makes 12 - 15.

crust:
  8 tablespoons butter, room temperature
  1 package (8 ounces) cream cheese, room
      temperature
  1 cup flour

filling:
  2 cups pecans, coarsely chopped
  ¾ cup brown sugar
  2 eggs
  1 teaspoon vanilla
  1 tablespoon bourbon
  2 tablespoons corn syrup

mini pecan pies

Mix crust ingredients and fill greased mini tart pans, making
   crusts that cover indentions completely.
Fill crusts with pecans to the top.
Mix remaining filling ingredients and add to tarts, spooning
   about a tablespoon full in each.
Bake in 350-degree oven for 15 - 20 minutes.
Let cool completely before removing from pan.
Makes 15 - 18.

crust:
  16 tablespoons butter, room temperature
  2 cups flour
  ¾ cup brown sugar
  1 cup walnuts, chopped

filling:
  1 package (8 ounces) cream cheese, room
      temperature
  1 teaspoon vanilla extract
  1 cup sugar
  1 tub (12 ounces) Cool Whip

topping:
  1 can (21 ounces) blueberry pie filling

blazin' blueberry

Combine crust ingredients and spread in a 13 x 9-inch
    greased glass casserole dish, firmly packing crust into
    the bottom of the dish.
Bake crust in 350-degree oven for 15 - 20 minutes and cool
    completely.
Mix filling ingredients and evenly spread filling on crust.
Evenly spread blueberry pie filling on top of Cool Whip
    layer.
Chill for at least 1 hour and serve.
Serves 12.

2 packages (16 ounces) cream cheese, room
    temperature
2 tablespoons butter, room temperature
¼ cup milk
1 cup sugar
8 medium flour tortillas
2 cups cooking oil

cannoli

Blend cream cheese, butter, milk, and sugar.
Place 4 tablespoons of mixture in center of tortilla.
Fold the side closest to you over the filling.
Fold the left and right sides inward.
Roll away from you until only ½ inch is exposed.
Spread a thin layer of filling on flap and continue rolling.
Freeze cannolis overnight.
Place oil in frying pan and heat oil over medium-high heat.
Fry cannolis until golden.
The center may still be cold.
Serve sliced in half.
Makes 16.

2 cups flour
2 cups sugar
1 teaspoon baking soda
1 teaspoon baking powder
2 teaspoons cinnamon
2 teaspoons nutmeg
¼ teaspoon salt
4 eggs
1½ cups oil
1 teaspoon vanilla
3 cups carrots, grated
½ cup pecans, coarsely chopped

triple carrot cake

In a large mixing bowl, mix flour, sugar, baking soda, baking
      powder, cinnamon, nutmeg, and salt.
In a large bowl, mix eggs, oil, and vanilla.
Slowly add dry ingredients to the large bowl.
Add carrots and pecans to mixture.
Pour mixture into greased 9 x 9-inch pan and bake in 350-
      degree oven for 45 minutes.
Serves 12.

½ cup cocoa
½ cup water, boiling
½ cup light beer
8 tablespoons butter, room temperature
1½ cups sugar
2 large eggs
½ cup evaporated milk
1 tablespoon vinegar
1 tablespoon vanilla extract
2 cups flour
½ tablespoon salt
1 tablespoon baking soda
1 tablespoon baking powder
2 cups chocolate chips

chocolate surprise

Mix cocoa with water in bowl until it is a smooth paste.
Add the beer and set aside to cool.
In another bowl, blend butter, sugar, and eggs until fluffy.
Then add evaporated milk, vinegar, and vanilla and mix well.
Add flour, salt, baking soda, baking powder, and cocoa
      mixture and mix until batter is smooth.
Then add chocolate chips and pour into a heavily greased 9 x
      13-inch baking pan or round cake pan and bake in
      350-degree oven for 40 - 45 minutes.
Serves 12.

½ cup shortening
1 egg
½ cup brown sugar
½ cup sugar
1 cup uncooked oatmeal
1 cup flour
1 cup cornflakes
1 cup Rice Krispies
1 teaspoon vanilla extract
½ teaspoon baking soda
½ teaspoon baking powder
¼ teaspoon salt

cereal cookies

Blend shortening, egg, and sugars well.
Combine remaining ingredients with mixture.
Shape into textured balls and place on greased cookie sheet
½ inch apart.
Bake in 350-degree oven for 12 - 15 minutes.
Makes 24.

1½ cups all-purpose flour
½ teaspoon baking soda
½ teaspoon salt
12 tablespoons butter, room temperature
½ cup sugar
½ cup brown sugar
1 egg
½ teaspoon vanilla extract
2 cups chocolate chips
½ cup peanut butter
4 different chocolate candy bars, chopped
1 small bag (1.74 ounces) M&Ms

pizza pie

Combine flour, baking soda, and salt.
Beat in butter, sugars, egg, and vanilla extract.
Stir in 1 cup of chocolate chips.
Spread batter onto a greased 12-inch pizza pan.
Bake in 375-degree oven for 20 - 25 minutes.
Immediately after removing from oven, sprinkle the
       remaining chips and spread peanut butter, swirling it
       with the melting chocolate chips.
Top with candy and serve.
Serves 12.

1 cup sugar
16 tablespoons butter, room temperature
2½ cups flour
1 egg
1 teaspoon rum
½ teaspoon salt
½ teaspoon vanilla extract

coffee cookies

Beat the sugar and butter in bowl until creamy.
Add other ingredients and mix well.
Place dough on wax paper or foil and roll into a log.
Freeze the log for ½ hour.
Slice the log into ½-inch thick slices and place on greased
       cookie sheet, 1 inch apart.
Bake in 350-degree oven for 15 minutes.
The cookies should not brown.
Makes 24.

1 box (10 ounces) Lorna Doone cookies
8 tablespoons butter, room temperature
½ gallon vanilla bean ice cream, soft
1 tub (12 ounces) Cool Whip
1 package (3.4 ounces) vanilla instant pudding
5 Heath candy bars, crushed
5 large Hershey chocolate candy bars, melted

classic party bowl

Mash Lorna Doones while combining with butter.
Place in a glass (trifle) serving bowl.
In a mixing bowl, combine ice cream, Cool Whip, and box of
    instant pudding.
Place half of the mixture over the cookie layer in the serving
    bowl.
Layer crushed Heath pieces over mixture.
Add remaining ice cream mixture over Heath pieces.
Pour melted chocolate bars to top the dessert.
Serves 12.

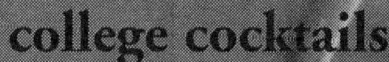

college cocktails

southern tea
½ tall glass of Lipton
   Southern Style iced tea
1 shot raspberry vodka
1 shot Southern Comfort
1 shot peach schnapps
fill with ice

blue ice
¾ glass Blue Ice
   Kool-Aid
⅓ glass vodka

appletini
½ apple schnapps
½ vodka

jungle juice
1 fifth Everclear
8 - 10 quarts Kool-Aid

winter mix
½ pint hard cider
½ pint of
   Guinness beer
   layered on top

Irish car bomb
½ shot Bailey's
   Irish Cream
½ shot Kahlua
drop shot in pint of
   Guinness beer

bibliography

Biggs, Fiona. *Simply Chicken*. (Parragon Publishing, 2001.)

Biggs, Fiona. *Simply Pasta and Italian*. (Parragon Publishing, 2001.)

"Consumer Advice on Food Safety." U.S. Food and Drug
    Administration, Center for Food Safety and Applied Nutrition. 1 May 2004.
    http://www.cfsan.fda.gov/~lrd/advice.html.

"Fact Sheets." U.S. Department of Agriculture, Food Safety
    and Inspection Service. 1 May 2004.
    http://www.fsis.usda.gov/Fact_Sheets/index.asp.

"Food Dictionary." Epicurious. 1 May 2004.
    http://eat.epicurious.com/dictionary/food/.

I gratefully acknowledge the food critics that helped test these recipes:

James Abruzzino
Andrew Fletcher
Brandon Fletcher
Irene St. George
Kristi Laurenz
Lane McBride
Robert Smith

&

editor:

Kristi Laurenz

index

0-595-66552-7